MADNESS

MADNESS

by GABRIEL OJEDA-SAGUÉ

NIGHTBOAT BOOKS

New York

ISBN: 978-1-64362-117-3

Design and typesetting by Joel Gregory
Typeset in Adobe Caslon and Criterion

Cataloging-in-publication data is available
from the Library of Congress

Nightboat Books
New York

www.nightboat.org

the clearest sea,
where from on high, floating,
I can see my outline flowing by.

REINALDO ARENAS, "OH SOLE MIO"
TR. KELLY WASHBOURNE

Mosquitoes in flight
Tiny wings batting the air
Eggs into egg cream

KEVIN KILLIAN, "MOSQUITOES"

for Jibreel

Everything past this page is a fiction. All real parties and persons mentioned past this page did not act in the way they are described here. The reader will be informed when they can assume truth again.

MADNESS

THE SELECTED POEMS OF LUIS MONTES-TORRES
(1976-2035)

Edited by Javier de las Palmas
& Ángel de la Escoba

NIGHTBOAT BOOKS

New York

TABLE OF CONTENTS

SAILING   63
SINGRITO PRESS, 2013

DICTATION   77
QUIVERING DUVET PRESS, 2024

HOLD ME TO IT   97
HALF-LIFE BOOKS, 2028

INTRODUCTION

Luis Montes-Torres was like a knot in a muscle; Luis Montes-Torres was like a hole in fabric. Both seem to be true. An always-active, hardened node straining towards something that isn't there—or a little negative, an unwoven dot made by threads moving too far from each other or by some foreign object pushing its way through. He was a boring fire. This is the first selection of his poems, published twenty years after his death in 2035.

It was a question about immigrant environmentalisms, posed to us by a mentor and comrade of ours, that led us back to Montes-Torres's poetry: "do they work?" Do they work? To Ángel, this meant do they effect change in the world, do they reverberate? To Javier, this meant do they coalesce together, do they jell into anything like a philosophy? A prior research collaboration of ours on multilingual protest poetics brought Montes-Torres into our footnotes as a negative, one example among many of Cuban American poets writing exclusively in English. But we remembered later, on brainstorming how to wrap our heads around this question, the uneven breadth of Montes-Torres's work, the gestures and confusions he seemed to set out for us, towards these issues and more. We knew that his work seemed to know something, something useful, though it was unclear what exactly.

And so began our long, new relationship to a minor poet, one who briefly reached notoriety on being shortlisted for the National Book Award and on winning the Lambda Literary Award for his collection *The Ocean as It Shouldn't Be*, but who went almost entirely disregarded by the end of his life. As we moved through what we could find of his work, we noticed a pattern. Each piece of Montes-Torres's career that we encountered seemed disconnected from the others, each book uncomfortable with its place in his body of work, each critic of his only able to hold one book or one poem or one theme to analysis at a time. Our job, as we began to see it, was to be connective tissue. We decided, perhaps out of frustration, perhaps out of faith that there was indeed something there, to take on the task of organizing what we could find, of making for Montes-Torres a document that would turn this scatter into a line. This book is the result.

With a grant from the National Association of Latino Arts and Cultures and with the guidance of Montes-Torres's longtime partner, Evan Bower, we have been able to edit this selection of Montes-Torres's poetry. This book is arranged chronologically, selecting various poems from each of Montes-Torres's published books, presented in the order they originally appeared in. As well, among his poems, we have tried to build something of a biography for this still under-known poet. In brief notes before each selection of poems, we detail the events of his life that led to the publication of each book, his interlocutors at the time, and some frameworks for thinking about the contributions and consequences of his life for Latino-American poetics in the early 21st century.

His moves, his attachments, his fears, his moods—as much as these seem to thicken the meaning and context of his poetry, just as often these bits of his life deflate, confuse, or betray it. He was both frustratingly mild and dramatically reactive. He was a man of obsessions and anxiety, of interest and wonder. He was as much enchanted as disenchanted. We wanted to be stuck with Montes-Torres, stuck in the same way he was stuck, and we invite the reader to follow us there.

Javier de las Palmas & Ángel de la Escoba, 2055

HILLS AND TOWERS

HARD SHOT PRESS, 1996

EDITORS' NOTE

Luis Montes-Torres was born on June 28th of 1976 in Pinar del Río, Cuba. On May 10th, 1980, at just four years old, he was taken by his father, Javier Montes, on a ship to Key West as part of the Mariel boatlift, leaving his mother, Pilar Torres, in Cuba. His father would later recount that on their ship they sat next to Mirta Ojito, eventual Pulitzer Prize-winning journalist, and Julio González, eventual mass murderer. After a difficult sojourn in the Keys, Montes-Torres and his father took a series of buses from Florida to Fairfax, Virginia, where Montes-Torres grew up.

He attended English-language schools where his grades were poor and he had few friends, both due in large part to his initial difficulty with English. Even without much of a social circle through his education and adolescence, Montes-Torres was generally described by his family as a charming, energetic, and positive child. He collected insects, taught himself crochet, and watched movies to pass the time; he was boyish and handsome, though acne-prone and susceptible to chronic ear infections. After graduating from high school, he attended George Washington University for a single semester before dropping out in 1994. In a 2012 interview in *BOMB*, he cited "a boredom [he] could not find the bottom of" as the reason for his leaving the university so quickly.

A generally poor relationship with his father, the fact that he had not had contact with his mother since 1980, and his lack of close friends left Montes-Torres with very little financial support during his first years out of college. During that time, he worked for meager pay as a food prep assistant at a gallery in Washington, DC, where he became exposed to art and writing outside of school. In the same interview from 2012, Montes-Torres says of this time:

> There was so much I had to do to feel I had my feet on the ground anywhere in the world. I began a process of internal digging, hoping I would find an inner resource to

replace the joy of outside things, which had started to dull. But I didn't find anything inside of me. Art in my life was a temporary answer to an important question: what do I now care for?

Montes-Torres credits his first encounter with poetry as an adult to reading John Wieners's *Selected Poems* in 1994 at the recommendation of a gentleman who frequented the gallery. Evan Bower recalls: "Lu told me he used to cling to those patrons, play up his accent, and beg them for little gifts and things like that. If someone really recommended Wieners to him, it wasn't just out of appreciation for the arts."

Montes-Torres began writing his own poetry in late 1994. Initially, he attended a few local poetry readings in DC but socialized little and rarely performed his own work. In 1996, he sent a slim forty-five-page manuscript of a book he titled *Hills and Towers* to Hard Shot Press, a small anti-capitalist poetry press, where it was published in an edition of 150.

It seems like an obvious joke, but naming a book of poems after an English translation of his own last name may not have been intended as one by Montes-Torres. In fact, the critics who have written on Montes-Torres's first book note that this title could be, as Mark Weiss describes it, "an implicit recognition of his heavily anglophone literary tastes," or rather, what Ilan Stavans calls "the first sign of what would slowly morph into a cultural rejection, like an organ rejecting a host." But these critiques seem biased by knowledge of Montes-Torres's later work.

When *Hills and Towers* was published in 1996, publicity for the book was basically nonexistent. No reviews of the book ever materialized, and the first interview published with Montes-Torres would not appear until 1999. In fact, there may not have been much contemporary readership at all. In 2037, a box containing seventy-five copies was discovered in a distributor's warehouse in Illinois, unopened and untouched until then. With half of the published copies never leaving the warehouse, Montes-Torres and Hard Shot Press could have only sold or given away a maximum of seventy-five books around the time of publication. Whether because of Montes-Torres's small social circle and nascent reputation in poetics circles, or Hard Shot Press's lack of inspiration for marketing work, neither seemed to ever notice the missing stock.

Nevertheless, the poems that began Montes-Torres's career, while slimmer and less crafted than his next books, proved to him that he was able to produce worthy art of his own. The poems of *Hills and Towers* begin to chip at some of the questions that Montes-Torres's poetry troubles over so often, and they do it with a freeness that Montes-Torres rarely lets himself return to until his late work.

LEARNING

in the drainage basin
how to separate
my ideas from
each other
it's some difference
between rain
and small ponds
falling
just to ruin my clothes
to collect into each other
a hand on a
path towards
something perfect
there is a bush
with a small model
of the world confined
between leaves
the watershed turns inside out
something I'll
have to remember
I put a pencil
on the river
and draw it a source

HILLS AND TOWERS

and the smaller blessings
they reconfigure
laid bare and even
in front of them
it could be
thought by a
passerby
that the distance
is a nightmare but it is
always worth the
trek, making yourself
glimmer just
to get smaller
in that green
and shadowed
screen, it is always worth
it
to walk straight into
the background
and open your mouth

DESIGN

let's presume
there is a formula
to foliage
and someone
with their head on
straight could
dedicate life
to natural patterns
it might be unbelievable
giving yourself
room to
criticize
and hold
hands
I will drive a kite
into a leafy
branch
a bookmark
for lack
of a better word

MOTION

I said the boat is lonely
not me
it is tempting
to put a towel down
and stare
at the difference
that bee in its work is a flag
meant soon to be metallic
it could motion
a change in me

RIVER

bolts of fabric
can also be pulled
out of the river
dredged out
after someone has
reported them missing
silk and lace
can also watch
the river go by
sitting on the banks
reading
in muddy grass
yarn can also
evaporate
and rain
to fill yarn river
cotton can also
degrade a stone
over time
you can also throw
a soda can
into linen
you can pay
to clean it out
this dress
is running directly
into the ocean
chiffon, chiffon, chiffon

IN THE PARK

pretend with me
waving our arms
tangling our tongues
in the middle
of the park
designed unfortunately
just for this
I would like
to whisper to you
if you do not believe me
I am in control
you don't need
a phone
pass by me
this is a tree
we're pretending

poems are a single stream that turns and turns

PAINTING

there is a painting hanging
and a boat inside
of it and a dog
on the boat
I can find
out how
to narrate this
event
it is amazing
a dog on a boat
where is it going
what is the temperature
listen to me
I am promised
my life is a
story told by
molecules
we should let
the dog tell us
where we are going
and how to get there

trim
surprise

turn

OVER THE DESK

a comely pile of foam
at the top of my stairs
that has come
to cover me
what can't it explain
the knot at the base
of my back
no it can explain that
the movie in a
magnolia
the letter about
mudslides
it can only start
to slither down
the kiss
we traded
over the
desk
you said I was
being generous
in kissing you
no it can explain that

FLEW

where I'd
like to go
tonight
is for the
little red line
to know
I flew when
a car honked
I would ask you to decide
tonight what is
good about being
from Virginia
to put your ear
to the air
hear that
I'm singing over water
so it will
be carried everywhere
so it will trail everyone's houses
I don't like
being here
so I won't

IN THIS MODE

the fire escape
is an obvious
decoration
I want to jump
out of my apartment
into a premise
of skin against concrete
or skin against polyester
in piles
or against the red oak
planted as a sign
to indicate
the going of cars
this little jewel
gardened here
in this mode
of counting exhales
everything will take
much longer, the metal
stairs will be
a nervous
process
but descending them
they open, flower
and turn into chainmail

RAISE

I'm worth much
more than this seed bag
torn and spilled onto
K street
sure, an upside
down jungle
in fact
a rumor is going
around that I cannot
grow anything
outside of my hands
the pale pleasant
sky handle
the deep black
that must be in
the center of a seed
I give a box
of utensils
to my brother
because I know
that he can raise a family

ONE TOOL OF MANY

to stop from waking
up so suddenly in the
middle of the night
might be a mosquito
something to focus on
something that loves noise
or a receipt twitching
by an air vent
or a better dream
one worth seeing all
the way through
one where I am
surprised to see you
and a flower leans
one where the start
of the next day
is foretold
in letters
and is worth
it to postpone

AT AN ANGLE

BURNING DECK PRESS, 1999

EDITORS' NOTE

Holding on to newfound confidence gained from the publication of *Hills and Towers*, Luis Montes-Torres dedicated significant portions of his time in the late 90s to learning about and connecting with poets in the Northeast. He was buoyed by a sense of excitement and with that excitement came a new willingness to socialize, continuously invigorated by receiving recognition for his talent. Montes-Torres focused his attention on small experimental presses in the Northeast, including Burning Deck, Roof Books, Chax Press, Soft Skull, and Blast Off Books. Although he was too poor to travel much, he often wrote to poets whom he admired. Some remaining letters suggest that he held ongoing correspondence with poets like Gil Ott, Peter Gizzi, Rosmarie Waldrop, Elizabeth Willis, Edwin Torres, and Flavio Bona Regio.

The only reference in the surviving correspondence about the manuscript which would become *At an Angle* is from a letter to Edwin Torres in 1998, one year before the book's publication. Montes-Torres wrote, "Now that I am feeling more involved in this world, I am starting to think I must write as if there are several worlds on top of me. And I have been writing that way. As if I were measuring where I started and stopped. You are like this too, I know." *At an Angle* is composed of a long poem, describing the writing process of someone addressed in second person, and several shorter meditative pieces. Published in an edition of 300 by Burning Deck Press, *At an Angle* was Montes-Torres's first notable work, gaining him his first reviews and interviews, with a generous blurb from Barbara Guest.

Among readers, reactions and reviews were mixed to positive, but the book seemed at least to make an impression with the Waldrops and Burning Deck's regular readers. Charles Bernstein and Marjorie Perloff's 2011 collaborative essay on Burning Deck's history happens to mention *At an Angle*, citing it (incorrectly) as an example of the press's publication of works in translation. *At an Angle* signaled the arrival of a new poet with obvious merit—though still finding his voice—and ingratiated him with a handful of peers, mentors, and gatekeepers. But it's difficult to tell in this moment who Montes-Torres's audience was; not just who read him, but who he was writing for. His early work seems wrapped in itself, but he was slowly making his way towards having some attention paid to what he was doing.

Nevertheless, new friends and minor notability would not change Montes-Torres's living situation, as his low-paid part-time position at the gallery only barely kept him afloat. "Lu couldn't really keep a full-time job," Evan Bower told us, "It just wasn't easy for him. But when we first met he liked to defend that from some 'righteous poverty' thing. He ate a peanut butter and jelly sandwich for every day's lunch, half his dinners were canned and warmed on a hot plate. He'd say it was all he needed, that he liked to live simple. I never really believed that."

FROM "AT AN ANGLE"

you've seen yourself here before

a piece of paper with nothing on it

the ways you drift away

you've held your hand up to measure

painted drops of your memory

you think one idea you have now is useful

the most useful thought you've had today

but you are nervous and breathing

seems unbelievable, the opposite of expression

but you are supposed to write something down

pour distracted glances as hot metal into a mold

let a doctor show you your blindsight

the village swimming on candle wax

your time in this room is, to some, limited

use it, declaw blades of grass

every day this writing grows ironic

where it leads you and where it doesn't

where it seems to and where it shouldn't

it feels rare but it isn't

that smell is just your room

managing telepathic signals

a rune crudely drawn on your forehead

every step into love is one away from your mother tongue

and this dreamy moment is coded nation

an alarm in somebody else's home tells you

someone is past waking up, or should be

you'd like to reject this

you'd like to reject dying

maybe there's a thinner barrel of air

I don't mean to blind myself and chain monkey tails into stanzas

you might feel absent in your own room

but you are wrong

you keep being wrong automatically

when you set out to sculpt

to shrink the world in your eye

until it pops into runes

until it seems as small as steam

condensing on a white wall

your job is to draw an outline to a kingdom

and to be somewhere in its muddled populace

maybe a clue, a twist, but certainly a stone, a description

don't let this be so simple

a thin atmosphere of cologne

a star, someday, will be resting unopened on the table

it can be cracked by a hammer and made ordinary

if that incessant rumbling at the back of your throat persists

let a stranger stuff it back into your ribs

this is so you can focus in quiet

this is all so you can pass like a truck on a highway

from one white point to another white point

and dramatize it simply and terribly

the ink stain you've left is another country

floating

you are here to write a new book

and instead you are summoning fickle islands

you notice the fan is spinning lopsided

you shouldn't write that down

it gets easier

when the surface tension is broken

when your darkened back cracks wide

after a bird drops onto a power line

there is this stillness that makes itself concrete

beginning to be everywhere, like candy

a cat convincing itself it's hungry

to beg to be outside, to beg and choose

you'll peel the skinny image of leaves from their sound

hold them inches apart

to make a headache

the idea is hoping to freeze over

a permanent pill, a raised barrier

someone is speaking rapidly at the edge of the room

you turn to know, not to notice

sweat is piling on your paper

as you try to temper the rant and stop it from passing

through where the window starts and the wall stops

at an angle

this procrastinated page looks like a ribbon of snow

fallen on your island

which has never seen snow

causing some half-birthed blindness in its scared strangers

now they can act famous, play the cello

but you can feign preciousness

or you can rest your head on mine

this room is empty

so are you

you could scream and fill it quickly

over the minute of your lifetime

or you can rest your head on mine

and smell that grease in the air

that tells us strangers that it is about to rain

GARGOYLES

there are no secrets between us

except the spaces placed between us

it's impossible to lie now

as I wake up again

coughing

having to cook again

placing gargoyles for an audience

there's nothing but electricity between us

the vision of you in bed

five seconds behind the sound of you in bed

and the poem, another one

that comes from not knowing where else to go

nothing but a waterspout

to ward off spirits

and attract newer, sharper spirits

ALL THE LOVE BUSH

PINNED FLOWERS PRESS, 2002

EDITORS' NOTE

Evan Bower's role in the life and poetry of Luis Montes-Torres cannot be overstated. Montes-Torres and Bower met each other early in the year 2000 while walking around late at night on the George Mason University campus, where Bower was completing a graduate degree in bioinformatics. While we can't do much justice to a story of romance, let's just say that they quickly fell into habit with each other. *All the Love Bush* is the poet's tribute to the first years of their relationship, as they lived together in Bower's Adams Morgan flat. Quick to move in with each other, the pair lived together their entire relationship, moving from Washington DC to Los Angeles to Philadelphia. They were life partners until Montes-Torres's death in 2035.

The last book Montes-Torres wrote while living in DC, *All the Love Bush* was also the last book he wrote in relative obscurity, bringing a steadier and more interested audience to his continuing practice. Despite the long gap between the publication of *All the Love Bush* and the celebrated *The Ocean as It Shouldn't Be*, the writing in this earlier book is a clear precursor to the latter's more lyrical and formally conservative style. Though poet and paleontologist Donald Luckily called the style of *All the Love Bush* "formal and clean," Montes-Torres himself despised such a description. While a quick and curt style was valuable to the younger Montes-Torres, he had become by this point significantly more interested in poetic forms of structure and weight, which in their ordered composition could hold a variety of abstractions and allow for riskier images than those of his early work. Where this interest in mass and order in his poems was shaped into lyricism, sentimentality, and desire on subjects like love, difference, and the ordinary in *All the Love Bush*, *The Ocean as It Shouldn't Be*, and the unfortunate *Sailing*, it is transformed into an interest in excess and breakage with regards to environmental pollution and emotional exhaustion in later titles like *Dictation* and *Hold Me to It*. Mass becomes mess.

All the Love Bush was published in an edition of 500 by Pinned Flowers Press, a small but well-known gay and lesbian poetry press based in Little Rock, Arkansas. Montes-Torres had met its editors by chance through an unrelated Craigslist ad, but when both parties realized their shared work in poetry, discussions of publication blossomed.

ALL THE LOVE BUSH

I pretend: your galaxy, mine. But we
found the backside
of homemaking, made a trail
and followed it. We said weave
this pink antibiotic air into a bush.
Float there on me.

Inside,
there is a play we watch, women
singing songs. There is an eagle
in my eye, there is someone
to talk to. There is the place
where your hand draws weather. It's simple.
You said, "a cloud," you got one. I'm not fearing
light today. I'm covered in it.

And the book I
dreamed of, I wrote. My gathering
of fruit sending songs enough to follow
a plot. This evening, mercury nursery, will send
me a poem I won't hide. Take over
from here. Set me down
under our squeaking ceiling fan.

If you hear guitar notes, wave
the "Actually" away from both of us.

SPENDING

It must be like batteries,
spending this afternoon in a picture with you, both
of us wondering when every minute is, and how to find
our way back to them. Sure, we can take
the river there. We can open our mouths in front of
the window for the passersby. This spending
is the riddle "of" "all." What we make in every
method of passing, one after the other, the days.
Or, how we decorate them as we move. Maybe
I'm making the total nature of waiting into a parade,
but you'll have to excuse me. This is what I bury,
and how I know that something disappeared
is luxurious and able. Two hips joined
together is safe. I let my attention
be liquid when my head is resting
on your chest hair, the only time that
being physically real, being findable
by logic, doesn't scare me. So, we'll sew
an hour into another, admit
no one we know really is dying, just to
make the afternoon yawn, fizzle, spread, or spring.

CHASE SCENE

at night you stumble, dreaming
cross-eyed of a chase scene
three yellow wasps on your chest
the city you turned around in
a chase that quickly lands into a fight

the nagging anxiety of a stain somewhere
a tickle at the back of the throat
a song's bridge playing over and over in the head
maybe the stain is at the bottom of your lung
maybe this white crusting along the edge of the bed

I lay an icepack on your head
one of the old ones that look like a lazy waterdrop
unable to pop, I'm waiting for a more complete
courage, a peeled orange, a halogen lamp

believe it or not, we're recreating someone
from the 19th century's sin, by proceeding
mounted on the edge of our bed like
a permanent display, matching burdens
to caramels

the thin plant over the dresser is belonging here
you picture yourself with petals removed
and ask why you were not born gracious
I do a different dance in the same mirror

in the ultra-rendering of these buildings
I could snap my fingers
and every window would close
an accordion we accompany

EVAN SITTING IN THE CHAIR
THAT WRAPS HIM

Late energy makes the living
room seem like a lawn. This
light pressure on the uvula is
a holy ghost finger making us
aware of when to lay our heads
down. But we aren't there yet.

A mottled flower sneaks
over into his jeans while he's sitting in
the chair that wraps him. With my
sash on, "the syrupy skeleton
of storytelling," I am just looking.
Just telling him the differences
that came out of a spent day.
Went, did, saw, told, acted, thought.
And his—felt, did, was asked.

We take turns
as the statue on call, at the end
of depend. Fight off that white
noise worry. Turn the lamps on.
Let each other see, slowly
that there are only, and always,
two of us here.

TOOK A DAY

took a day to experiment on my thought
to arrange jars and wash clothes
to imagine being very moved by music
and then to be so

took a day to cool my hands
to give up the feeling in my stomach
that sometimes pushes me into playing the fool
to microwave rice

took a day to play cops and robbers with myself

a day where I find a little bug in my hair
a day where I forgive fretting
a day where I told everything else to wait

a day that ends
with how funny you look in your hat

WHEN I'M AFRAID WITH YOU

converting a cactus into a spray
when I'm afraid with you

convincing yarn to be kind to our animals
when I'm afraid with you

I stop biting on blue lights
when I'm afraid with you

you mince myth
when I'm afraid with you

covered in comfort, alone and together
when I'm afraid with you

careening and pearlescent, a moth, someone getting sick
when I'm afraid with you

I'd laugh too, rubber wonder, as lenient as I can be
when I'm afraid with you

phone never answered, shakes in spurts on concrete
when I'm afraid with you

"I don't know," easy to admit, thin air, touching your stomach
when I'm afraid with you

we stage the opera where I am Rodolfo
and you the delicate profile, unmoored, thrashing
and when I turn to you as I must
I sing "Line—Line—"

TENUTO

I am content as a minor poet
I can break a viola in three
the sound of dusk in wood grain
the easy hurting in the melody

so goes my semi-ironic attachment to all classical music

this recognition is what makes me start to cry
at a measure arranged into tenderness
I cry because I have so much to say

when you look over at me to see all this guessing
all this uncollecting, all this tenuto,
and the summer on my mind
the sometimes sudden miskeeping of others on my mind
be aware I'm in an orchestrated disturbance
a genie I fail to put up with
I can be pulled out
if maybe by a kick
or a tap of the ring finger on the collarbone

PROJECT

The evenly spread pleasure of waiting.
It's a soft bit of shelter, as a faint
sheen of silver passes overhead.

We suspect we have been mistaken
for someone else when we're desired,
someone who must look just like us,
but steadier, easier to talk to, kinder to waiting.
Out of the corner of my eye,
I think it must still be spring.

I heard what you meant to say,
that leaving things this way would hurt
too much. It just rose off of you.
And this must be what implication is: shine;
Closing your eyes to the sun and seeing red.

I hold someone's hand, I hardly think to breathe.
We unwrap this light and ask simple questions.
We think what our impatience is like,
together and not together.

The weather doubles the size
of the earth it falls on, like a projector,
like a shared secret. I promise not to sleep.
There is something outdated already
about this flower, tentatively growing, collapsible
into courtesy and airsickness.

OBSESSIONS

Obsessed with
how long it takes
for a glacier to melt
or a movie to end.

Taste of cream soda
all I think about
in the afternoons.

You pass a finger between
one tattoo and another,
find that I cannot make amends
with every copper thread between my ears.

I believe too much in spinning around.
I plant matches and pray for a forest.

When I am a creature soaked,
ride on my back,
ride on my back.

HOW I STOP

Seeing yourself and believing you
dreamed it is this feeling, a swallowed
one. I keep thinking,
of every ounce of disaster
these months. Awful feeling,
sitting, depending. Hands soaking
in melted butter. Grey films
shined onto the screen. It is
as bad as it gets then. But,
if I may, warmth opens forward,
remodels the naïve,
lets the two of us finally be quiet
and merely hopeful. A
seed of with, that loves to be.
I could pay good money for
that feeling, I could give to you,
give to you, and never take, or
we could yield to a darkened
theater and let it blush
as it's bound to do.

AN ILLUSTRATION

if the note I left you was enough
you'll see soon I'm asking only
for the last bit of a circle
the solar edge to be special
I'm asking only for that splashed nervousness
of our first day and the joy
of the rest passing in
simple eager celebration
tomorrow we'll perform that miracle again
tomorrow we'll see how certain
we can be, I'm asking you,
if the note was softly dropped in leather,
if the tender end of a stem is a ring,
if one seashell is like another,
to send this event over your shoulder,
to love me every day,
and to know every repetition is
a little ghost of me waving
from an echo

THE OCEAN AS IT SHOULDN'T BE

SINGRITO PRESS, 2011

EDITORS' NOTE

After the release of *All the Love Bush*, Montes-Torres fell into a writing slump. In 2004, at twenty-eight years old, Montes-Torres and his partner Evan Bower left Washington DC for Los Angeles, where they would live together for over a decade. While the impetus for the move had been a job offer for Bower, Montes-Torres was able to find part-time work in a local library. From 2004-2008, he also worked freelance jobs writing copy for kitchen appliance instruction manuals. While more work and a steadier income made life easier for the couple, it also meant less time for personal writing. We've been able to find a few paper drafts of poems from the period between 2004-2009, but none ever saw publication.

One major exception is a poem called "In the Morning." Millions of people who have never read Montes-Torres's work or even a book of poetry in their lives have read "In the Morning." That's because, in 2006, the cereal company Kellogg's marketing team held a poetry contest to help market Frosted Mini-Wheats, which were reaching record low sales. During the month of June 2006, Kellogg accepted submissions of poems, ten lines or less, about "why you love Frosted Mini-Wheats." The contest seemed to be intended for children, but Montes-Torres was the only person who submitted at all. His four-line poem "In the Morning" won the contest by default and was subsequently included on all boxes of Frosted Mini-Wheats for three months:

> the sight of white
> in the morning
> is a miracle
> Frosted Mini-Wheats

A poem on the side of a cereal box is the kind of thing people only read in bouts of concentrated boredom, so though he had exponentially more exposure than ever before, it was all a bit incidental. Kellogg's would later that year adapt the poem into their existing tagline, without Montes-Torres's consent, leading to Frosted Mini-Wheats being labeled with "the sight of white, crunch in every bite" until 2028 when the Kellogg's corporation permanently dissolved.

By 2009, the book that would become *The Ocean as It Shouldn't Be* was in production. It seems that living in Los Angeles, with its high Latino population, provided Montes-Torres with a better environment to consider his ethnic identity. *The Ocean as It Shouldn't Be* is certainly the work that most explicitly reckons with cultural experience, but its method and effectiveness have long been a subject of debate. When the book was released by Imelda Suarez's Singrito Press in 2011, it was considered an honest look at exile identity and the experience of the Marielitos. It garnered both American and international readers, was quickly translated into Spanish, and was considered an insightful personal narrative about immigration into the U.S. and the difficulties of culture shock.

However, twenty years after its publication, in February 2029, Montes-Torres denounced the book in a widely-watched DODO drop, saying that it was part parody, part potboiler, and a failure of a book on all levels. He remarked that the book was something between a send-up and an attempt to fit in. The drop is often confusing, historically inaccurate, and filled with self-deprecating remarks, but some of the points made in it do seem to resonate with *The Ocean as It Shouldn't Be*'s take on Latinidad. The sheer difference between his treatment of the issue of race in this book and its treatment in his other books is enough to make readers suspect that there may be some kind of irony or gimmick. In the years after the book's publication, it received accusations of insincerity and cliché, but they never came so explicitly, nor from the author himself, particularly considering that, for many years after its release, Montes-Torres swore by the book as his manifesto on Mariel and the exile.

Perhaps because both of us find our main interest in Montes-Torres's late ecological work, we aren't quite sure what to do with the cultural knots summoned by this book. Other scholars have done a better job of accounting for this book than we can here (see Ilan Stavans and

Iván Jakšić's 2023 book *What is el oceano?: A conversation*), but we tend to keep Montes-Torres's late career denouncement at arm's length. Frankly, his comments seem a product of an unwillingness to recognize his younger self's genuine investment in the book's style. While it's true that *The Ocean as It Shouldn't Be* seems ambivalent on the issue of poetry's relationship to ethnicity, we would be hard-pressed not to admit that it does feel like a relatively natural, if not particularly satisfying, product of his early work's formal concerns. His interest in the lyric, the simile, the non-sequitur, the ordinary, and forms of difference are all still here—just flatter, more conventional.

The Ocean as It Shouldn't Be was written quickly and handed to Singrito Press for publication in 2010. Editor Imelda Suarez, whose press was well decorated in the major awards by its closing in 2023, had a developed ability to move books into the right hands and Montes-Torres's was soon recognized with several literary awards. It was longlisted for the Lenore Marshall Poetry Prize, shortlisted for the National Book Award, and won both the Lambda Literary Gay Poetry Award and the Chancleta Prize for Original Latino Poetry. Montes-Torres became a public figure for the first time. These were his first and last awards in poetry.

DUE HERE

Think a wave above the wave,
What the authorities call an overload.

An official says "I haven't the foggiest
Notion of what will happen then"

As if we do, as if we weren't the fog itself.
Miami says it is already at its "breaking point,"

So we break it. We'll break it again.
We are crossing into a state of emergency,

Of a shattered record, of rented medical facilities
And portable toilets, of bus tickets if you're lucky.

It is one thing to be expected, another to be due.

AS IT WERE

We were stains in motion, a pattern of ships
Believing the wind could finally bless us
With something. Something, *Papá* said,
That your *madre* could never want,
Couldn't understand because she was heartless.

Many days, I also feel heartless here.
Just ash, a bit of cold water
On the forehead. We could have been
Unprincipled if we had just stayed
In the water forever.

We were stains in the water, as it were,
Signs that the land was bleeding.
We were sounds, as it were,
A rhythm and a rendition.
We were changing color, as it were,
The painting of suspended light.

MIRADA

Stones left along the road:
Somewhere design is being rejected;

An exercise for tuning:
Allow the route and the dream in turning;

Look at me on the side of the road:
Learning to lean on my knack for division;

Instead of that sing us this:
Inventions we never imagined;

Allow me an image:
An hutia and a crocodile in absentia;

Now as I am pulled apart by sound:
Navigate this side back to mother;

This side to a planned demolition:
The remains will sign the paperwork;

In this country, touch has patterned me:
Pollution, pale answers, mind's fire, panoply.

OF RECORD

What is of record is the heat as we already
Know it, the several silent moments between us

As the water swings lower than it should, as if
We were meant to sink without drowning.

What is of record is the ocean as it
Shouldn't be, but is, an adhesive

Road towards a puzzle box. This
Ossified cabinet stuffed with

Misfired desire can be
Received into data.

Papá answers where
We are with "here"

And he's exactly right,
Though he is setting us

Aside. Land us, and you will see
A transformation into allotropy.

SCUM

It would be easy to peel each boat
Off of the surface of the water,
Lift each into the sky,
And watch them dissolve.

It's no surprise we're called *escoria*
At home, scum here,
Prisoners, criminals,
Crowding your classrooms,

The ones that gave up,
The bits that were boiled out.
On both strips of land
They push us back into the water

Where we float until we're scraped off.
See this scum learn to chant
In a language that is less
Than its constituent parts.

SPELL

Then comes a change over me,
Turning at each joint
In the sidewalk, all objects
New, imagined in this enclosure.

Strangers observe
My body in belief
That it forecasts weather.
I catch all lies.

I lend two secrets as
Natural consequence to
The commotion I make
Passing on the road:

That the scabs along my wrists
Tell time, that every
Once perfect thought I have
Is lost as heat.

I keep another close
At hand: the power that "stay"
Has always had over me.

PLAY

What I first noticed
Waking up in Virginia
Was nobody acting.

Staid dialogue
Not delivered
But guaranteed.

I was guarded and melodramatic.
I was called by boys into playfulness

But disassembled
For my tongue's
Reliance on script.

Seen as a maquette
Towards a life,
Sloppy and obvious.

Every day I have no new thoughts,
Only acts following each other without pause.

GUSANO

I force your nose into the dirt
Asking,
Who in the world would want to be us?

If you move dirt in the right way,
Como gusano,
It stops looking like the simulation of dirt,

The spell you are under,
And begins
To look like dirt, the texture

We can think in,
Have to.
Next time you speak

In my tongue,
Fulano,
Remember I'm moving under your soles

Through foul architecture,
Holding
In my teeth an idea

Of how to make it all
Slip out
From under you to engulf you.

IN PILES

Juggling passwords between our mouths,
I connect to the men of American cities.

By runes, confession, dramatics,
I make them cry for a fruit
Whose name has been forgotten.

If they picture me in a puddle or in a wedding dress,
They become obsessed with snowfall.

One tabulates the words the other does not know,
Records his disappointments in spots
Along the thigh, velveteen.

Where is desire? In desire,
In leaves swept below a cassock.

We set our eyes on each other and our minds
On something else, make impossible shapes
In piles of fabric.

Do not ask me to repeat myself. Little matters
In this invention. Yours, mine, the one that shatters.

FLUSH

How long does it take
For the idea that the water is getting darker,
Thinner, to pass between twelve people
Touching shoulder to shoulder?

Alongside flushed car parts, an opera singer disappears
As steam over the sea.

SAILING

SINGRITO PRESS, 2013

EDITORS' NOTE

Imelda Suarez called Montes-Torres in December 2012, during the height of the success of *The Ocean as It Shouldn't Be*, to say Singrito would publish whatever manuscript he was currently working on. Though Suarez's desire to continue their success together was understandable, it's likely that both she and Montes-Torres would eventually agree that that request came too early. Montes-Torres didn't have a manuscript in progress when Suarez called him, but in the pressure of the moment, he lied and said that he did, asking for another month to finish it. Throughout January of 2013, Montes-Torres wrote *Sailing* in its entirety. It appeared in print not six months later.

This would be the first time Montes-Torres wrote following somebody else's timeline. It's a temporary aberration in his otherwise freeform writing life, and one that doesn't go particularly well. Because he hadn't prepared a concept for the next book, he decided to "copy the last one," to use his own words. *Sailing* ended up as a weak echo of the themes of *The Ocean as It Shouldn't Be*, with little to no originality or shine. Its imagery is clumsy, its messages confusing, and its style clichéd.

The most unfortunate thing about *Sailing* was its timing. One bad book in a writer's career is nothing particularly surprising, but coming so quickly after such a hit made many think of Montes-Torres's former success as an accident. He suddenly became a one-hit wonder. Readers who doubted Montes-Torres's talent and staying power were given all the more reason to disqualify him, and even some of his consistent readers began to believe that his career was waning.

Sailing is held in such low regard that virtually none of the poems within it are remembered, quoted, taught, or included in anthologies. Therefore, we've decided not to include any of *Sailing* in this selection of Montes-Torres's work. In its place, we are publishing here two excerpts from Montes-Torres's diaries, covering the full extent of the years 2013, the year of publication of *Sailing*, and 2024, the year of publication of his next book, *Dictation*. Montes-Torres's diaries have a particular style, written in extremely short, mostly daily entries. They record his mood, what he was reading, stray observations, and ongoing frustrations. No entry is longer than a paragraph and most entries are as short as a sentence. For ease of reading, we've chosen to remove dating and organize these entries by dividing each day with a pipe. Any blank spaces between pipes indicate a day where there was no entry.

EXCERPTS FROM THE DIARIES OF LUIS MONTES-TORRES (2013 AND 2024)

2013

Am getting into running, at the behest of a friend who I do not have time to talk about here. | Today incredible sky. | Keep thinking every song I hear perfectly describes my life. It is a sign of a bad week. | Newscasts hard to watch. | Skateboarder on the street looked exactly like Evan. | New book is not working yet. Figuring out how to change its rhythm. | Today am having much empathy for younger versions of myself. Evan says I should try to do things that make me feel like me but, well, that's the problem. | Today saw the best dog. It is important to be able to tell what is cute in this world. | Yesterday was less good than I thought, now that I am doing today. Which is to say, today is good, but I am doing too much thinking about yesterday. | Is invention possible? | Today believed I saw my brother in the mirror, but I do not have a brother. | Sailing coming along badly but quickly. Do not know what to write but am writing. Reading in a week in Chicago. | | | Today I am writing while on a plane. Thinner thoughts, better poems. | Cannot stop thinking about the phrase "explosive road" which I have made up today and the Berssenbrugge line "a single emotional line of one self in one time, like a wind that comes up." | I am easily attached. | Reading was okay. Felt lonely. Turnout was good. Forgot to buy the other reader's book but I liked her. | | | | Have been better. | Today totally grey. Read a lot. | Am considering finding a relationship with my mother again. Might be a bad idea. | Wish I played the clarinet! But happy today otherwise. | Finished Sailing today and sent it to Imelda. I must stop writing the same book over and over again. Passed this one out of me as if through a sieve. Feel unsure about it. | Could kiss Evan for hours. | Imelda seems happy with Sailing. She wants to put "Lever" on the back cover instead of blurbs, because she says it is good. She knows better than me. | Imelda changed her mind and wants Martín Espada to blurb it. I asked her if it would be confusing since he is from Puerto Rico. Americans do not know much about difference. She says confusion helps sometimes. It has helped me many times. | My recurring dreams: 1) reading a book that feels magical to speak out loud but has no meaning 2) choking my father 3) being stuck back in high school. Had the first one of these last night. That book is amazing. | | Espada said yes. Would love to be named "sword." | Evan bought a shirt today that makes him look like a waiter. I told him so, but he says he likes it. | | | | Do not miss Virginia winters. 68 degrees today in LA. Thank god. | | Sailing coming in June. Fast. | | Today I feel like a videotape. | Am I a good writer? | Saw an air show today and enjoyed it, but now I keep imagining them crashing. Trying to turn that off. | Do frames matter that much in visual art? Lecture on frames today at the library and am still not certain. | | | | | | | | | | | | | | | | | | | | | | | | | | | | | | | | | | | | | | | | | | | | | | | | | | | | | | | | | | | | | | | | | | | | | | | | | | | | | | | | | Sorry was very busy. Will get back into the habit. | One of those days where I am totally listless but for just one moment, I see everything very clearly. | Today I imagined flight in many forms. | Wrote a poem today and I liked it. | Deleted the poem from yesterday. | When I die, I want to crackle about. | | On some streets of this city, I feel like I get hives. | I think my questions about boats are getting boring. | Evan and I spent all of today at a museum where I saw the most beautiful painting I have ever seen in my life. I don't remember what it was called. Evan is obsessed with Rothko. | One of those days where Evan and I took up space as if it was a way of communicating with each other. | The weekend felt like a small victory. Pet a dog today. | At night, I do not believe in anyone. | | | Have a friend I am in love with, but I am in love with many, many men. Sometimes I hit myself on the head to relax. Things are complicated. | At work today I watched a couple movies. It was a slow day. Waiting for Guffman and Some Like It Hot. Sometimes, I am like a dislocated shoulder. | Today sky perfect and, for an hour, pink. | After much deliberation, I have decided music is better for other people than me. | I have little to say today. Bought yarn. | Tried making visual art today. Made me happy. | | | From my apartment, I heard someone on the street getting hurt. | Went to the beach with Evan. I explained why I say the Pacific Ocean is a hallucination of the Atlantic. He laughed and tossed sand on my nose. | Great dog today. Brown and black and playful. | Read Schuyler on the way to work. Life is impossible. | | | I brought my friend lemonade today because she is down. | The rain today was a gift. | Read today in Los Feliz with three others. Many good poets here. Terrible wine at the reading. | Slow morning from the weed last night. Breakfast of rice, eggs, adobo. | Nikki Giovanni line: "I turned myself into myself." | Lecture on recycling plastic at the library. Thought about my toothbrush. | Tomorrow we launch Sailing in LA, then two days after in NY. Think I have figured out finally how best to read "At Rest" and "In a Bottle." Slanted and sagging, that is the secret. | | | | | | Sales are okay. Do not feel I have much energy to market it. Imelda is doing her best. | | Hate chihuahuas. Saw three today. Saw a cute pit bull. Refreshing. | Dayana does not like the book. I can tell. | The weather predictions were exactly right. | Saw Elliot today for the first time in weeks. He made some time for him and I to be alone. I told him all I wanted was his forgiveness, though I feel I am owed much more. Sometimes, I think I am driven to an embarrassing madness by men. With Elliot, with many other men, I feel as if I become a yearning and a talent for tenderness. Tenderness, as in, being easily chewed. | | | | | | | | | | Should stop writing my name on books I own. | "Conditions of possibility," who first said that? | The light in this apartment. A miracle on certain days! | At this point, I am so deeply rooted in Evan. Though there are days when I would like to run away, there are also days when I feel attached to any object he touches. | | Need to remember groceries and a good run today. | Richard Blanco and I had coffee today. Haha. He is very nice to look at. Bad poet though. | Reading Euripides in bed for a better portion of the day. | I am thirty-seven today. Wish we had pets. | Dream last night: in a field, I am standing. I apologize to someone I do not see and I begin to fly. | Some things I am thankful for today: the coffee Evan makes, 75 degrees, Spicer's After Lorca, Evan's recurring jokes, the Pacific Ocean, that the frisbee tossed by college kids missed my head, that my stomach has settled a bit, Fania All-

Stars, a nighttime drive with my friend. | Over eggs, my friend of many years said, "you forget sometimes that there are other people around you." The opposite of the problem, I think. But I know what she means. | | | | | | | | | | | | | | | | | | | | | | | | | | | | | | | | | | | | | | | | | | | | | | | | | | | | | | | | | | | | | | | | | | | | | | | | | | | Every year, September's coming surprises me. | DH Lawrence: "There is a sticky universal pitch that I refuse to touch." | Traffic so awful today I almost got out of the car to sit on my hood. Wanted to yell the whole way home. | | With a friend today who moved five years ago from Venezuela. We went out to the movies. At some point I made a joke to which she responded, "That's because you're American." When did I become the American? | Do I believe in ghosts? | Saw the tallest dog I have ever seen today. Amazing! | Today I felt like a very young version of me. Not a bad thing, this time. I felt like a version of me that recovers. | Impossible to compare brands of cereal on most days. | | Evan is sleeping and I am trying to learn how to play the guitar. | A child at the park today told me I was "very handsome." | | Helped Renata build a deck chair today. Who would have thought? Me! I think it turned out alright. | Maybe I would be like this in any country. | Increasingly convinced I have very much in common with dandelions, though I know I sound like a sissy when I say that. | At a farmer's market today with Evan and did not find cubanelle peppers. I told Evan it would be better if he just made porkchops for Renata instead. | | | Tonight, drank. | At the library I found a book of spells and thought something similar might make for a good next book. Must abandon this boats theme. | | Tonight saw Elliot, who apologized to me. It felt good to hear that. I'd been waiting for it. We sat in silence for a few minutes after. Felt like strings were pulling me towards him, though I didn't move. I hate this familiar feeling: potential energy. | Somewhere, someone in another country is playing soccer. Somewhere, someone in another country is thinking of naming their child Luis. | | | | At the beach with Evan, I swore the ocean and him were made of the same incredible yarn. | Wish I made more money, but the library and writing is all the stress I can handle. Though I have always been depressed, the last few years have brought me a certain fragility I cannot put my finger on. Fragility not that I will hurt myself, I have never fantasized that, too afraid of dying to do so. Fragile, as in, dedicated to a version of the world that does not hold under pressure. | | I laughed at everything Evan said tonight over dinner. We are hiking tomorrow. | | On the phone with Imelda I thanked her so much, even though the book is impressing few people. Wish I thought like her. | | This week Evan and I are watching every Stepford Wives movie. Three made for TV that we found online and two real movies. Tonight, watched the original. Katharine Ross is so very beautiful. | At lunch with my friend today, I had so much to say to her. | Writing in a café today something new. Poems about the weather, but I think they are convincing. | Had to abandon the Stepford Wives project halfway through. All terrible after the first one! | Today, there was an hour where the sky was acid yellow. I'm not sure why, and I don't think it was good. But it was very beautiful. | Corgi on the street today. | Leaves changing, even here. | | | | When I was a teenager, I had many dreams where I got sick and my mother came to take care of me. Last night, I had a variation of the dream: my mother was sick and my father was taking care of her. I was in New York, for some reason I can't figure out. | | | Read today with Francisco Amado Gonzalez and Hilda Inez. Why is it that even in my proper place I sometimes feel like someone's hallucination? When I feel most abstract is when I feel most nostalgic. | Today, I sat in the park to center myself, to feel less sad. A sparrow landed near me. Sparrows rarely sit for long. This one hopped around my feet for a while. | I have good weeks, sometimes. | I bought Evan a gold bangle today, which he said he likes because it makes him look like Cleopatra. I think he looks nice as Cleopatra. | If I could, I would give up everything, drive deep into the desert and sing until I couldn't anymore. Then, I'd soon be a cactus and a fox. | | | | | | | | We dressed as Bert and Ernie to Evan's friend's party. I had a bit too much tequila. | | | | | | | | | | Glück line: "Jack's bent elbow made me wistful for bending elbows." | Tried several times to end a new poem like the Hopkins poem that ends "ah! bright wings" but nothing sounded right. Exhale, with a tail. Ah! Bright wings! | Pretty nice day today. Even in this heat wave, Evan and I took some time to just walk around the neighborhood together. | | | | | | Dreamed of melted snow and serpents. | The focused look a man gives me on the street at night. Invitation or threat? Either way, in that look, the promise that I will be disassembled. | Dreamed of melted snow, serpents, tennis, baking soda, spray paint, damask, a patient in a bed. Dreamed a bay full of liquid silver. Dreamed my blood was water. Hard to focus today. | Better today. For me, the days after bad dreams have always felt like Ziploc bags. Went for a long run. | | | | | | | | | | | What right do I have to endlessly vacillate between feeling crummy and feeling in awe? | | | | | | | | | | | | | My mother's birthday. Have decided to finally write her. I often feel that many of my problems are caused by my life-long disconnect from my mother. Evan says that is unfair. Got an address for her from a distant cousin. I plan on telling her very little about my life. | | | I rarely feel nostalgic for DC, but I do miss the snow. To be more precise, I miss the first snow. | | | Every few days, I think Evan is a miracle. | | | Woke up and made Evan eggs. He spent a few hours of the morning calling family members. I bought myself a yo-yo, but I am not very good at it. | | | I use the water at the beach as a tuning fork. I flick it and try to set my brain to its pitch. | | Evan said to write down my New Year's resolution, so here: in writing, scare myself; in life, find and give safety.

2024

Woke up so thirsty. Slow morning. | Evan says the new year should be a chance at being better citizens of the world. Told him that was on corporations. Told him I loved him. | | | Putting a brick wall, metaphorically speaking, between me and my recycled images. | | | Watching movies when it isn't even cold out. | | Could I grow out my nails? | Evan found me in the worst of moods but set me straight. | Stayed with Puppet all day, who would not stop barking at the smoke. Waiting for when I will be open to new ideas. | Weed tonight feels bad, drowsy and detached. Getting doubts about the mush-rooms next week. | | At the supermarket, tore down a display. Felt like a kid. | | All the parked sailboats. Fingers in a fist. | Need to be drinking more water. | Surprised at how many minor frustrations occur during the end of the world. Mark cancelled brunch because of the smoke. | | | Went out to put my index finger on a tree. | Pup-pet's birthday. Bought him a bowtie. Evan bought him something he actually enjoys. | Asked Evan what he'd think if I didn't have a penis and he said "not much." I told him, for now, I wanted to learn to play chess. | | Thought to buy Evan this gadget he keeps talking about. You point it at a plant and it tells you if the plant is sick, what it has, and how to treat it. Surprisingly cheap. | | | | | When Alan said he wanted to be bodiless and just like an idea passed between people, I said I'd like to turn myself off and just sense, rotate and sense until I dug a deep ditch in the dirt. Alan is as dispirited with himself and the world as I am, so I sometimes invite him over for tequila. | | | Puppet loves me. Evan loves me. I love every bird I've ever seen. | | Must remember "eggshell" paint for guest room. And clouds tomor-row, definitely. | Want to learn how to cook meat better but should eat less of it anyways. | 37th day of fire here. So many people have left. When I close my eyes, I see myself either setting the fire or burning alive in it. Sometimes when someone is talking, I can't get such pictures out of my mind. I let them pass over me. I let them almost take me over. | | | | Kevin Killian line: "Big soft factory and / rubber belts on your pretty tan line." | Evacuated from where I was evacuated to. | | | Dreamed tonight of a palace with wood in the windows. | | | | After a long talk with Evan I think I am going to publish Dictation. I don't think it belongs anywhere, but I am going to put it there. Over these last three years repetition has kept me interested, but I worry it makes me look like Jack Nicholson in The Shining, whatever his name was in that. Jack. | | | | Have cut 100 pages of Dictation, easier done than you'd think. It is now 370 pages, which seems healthier. | Starting small again, want no more than a few hundred of these printed, if anyone takes it. | | | Am trying to pick up flossing, which is embarrassingly late for my age. | Nobody knows anything in the government or about it. | | | | | | Evan is imagining apples in flight. | These damn people in this damn city. All the time. | Had to stop on the middle of the highway today, I felt incredibly nervous. I stayed on the shoulder there a half hour before starting again. | If anything new is possible, I hope some plants grow. | | | | | | | | | | | | | | | | | | | | | | | | | | | | Rain tomorrow it seems. Thank god. | Purposefully left on the bathroom light for Puppet. It annoyed Evan, but I am less clumsy than I seem. | Laundry today and can use the line again. | "No hard feelings." Ha! | Met someone today who runs a press and wants a book from me. Told her about Dictation and she said, "don't send me 400 pages, but send me something." | Puppet dreams often and shakes his back legs. | I know Ezel hates me and is lying. | Saw Ezel, which was nice. | | | My Italian has gotten worse, I notice. | Is fog easier? | Ran my knee into a wall and had to see a doctor. | Evan's job offers him free lunches, but only catered salads that have these terrible looking cherry tomatoes. | Too old to be called a fag on the street, somehow no excuse. | Plane passed low. | | | | | Sent Mia 300 pages today. | Am embarrassed to write this, especially after Evan and I have argued all day about it, but I was in a fight with a man on the bus. I lost, maybe obviously. He was a little smaller than me and reminded me of Ezel. My knee now just feels much worse. | Ice every thirty minutes. Puppet licking my feet. | | | | | | | | | | | | | | Evan forgives me. He dyed his hair with henna and now he looks like a calico cat. | Mia advises edits. | At the beach, looking out at something I could not fully make out, must have been a ship, Evan explained prions to me. | | | | | | I fold my arms and then unfold them. | Someone I have not seen in many years, a regular patron at the gallery in DC, saw me in K-Town. We talked, very briefly, and he asked me if I still wrote. I told him no, mostly because I thought it was funny to say no. | Am looking at water from on a bridge. I feel I am getting dizzy. | Weather in reverse. | *In situ. In silico.* | | | | | | | | | | | Puppet outside. Evan asleep. Easier day. | Doc says, "Imagine if people really acted the way you fear they do." | You hear what they're doing in the rainforest and think yeah they want us dead. Them too. They must. They would do anything for death. | | | | | | Should I try sculpture? I think I would be good at it. | Imagined myself very sick and what my friends would say. | | | Dictation printing in September. I am very nervous. Evan is overjoyed. | Puppet looks younger every day. | Argued with someone at the Marxist reading group. | Why does Evan always act like this? | I must move out of this city always threatening to burn up. | | | | | | | | Spent the day decoding the messages Puppet sends to sparrows that run from him. | | | Am forty-five today. Could that be half? | I miss running. Better said, I miss running being easy. | Today I was very guarded to my friends. Tomorrow, I am going to eat a peach. | Doc says things being exactly the same enrages me. I say different. | Beach was packed with people and the sand was surprisingly cool on my feet. Watched a seagull steal Doritos. | Evan looking for new work. I brushed his hair while he napped. | Carmen called to wish me well. | | | | | In new forms, I am loaning miracles. | Reinaldo Arenas line: "the bonfire that will come to blot it out." | Today bought eggs to make eggs in the mornings. | Puppet and I running in circles. | I breathed deep and felt something sharp, acidic. | Woke up with a fever and believed I saw a gardenia growing from Evan's head. | My life sometimes feels like a record of the deaths of other things. Species, people. I see it until I am. We barely predicted what would happen to the coast of Georgia, to California, to the Philippines, to Vietnam, and yet we did and now look.| Bought a snow globe on a whim to decorate the dresser. | Must drink more water. | I am alive at the same time as that hummingbird! | | | | | | My impression of Charo is getting very good the more I learn to play the guitar. | Anything close together in Los Angeles feels like it was really meant to be. | Was in a fight again, with a man at the mall. In the doghouse with Evan. | Today fixed a flickering light. | Ill-advised to take vacation now, but Doc recommends as little social interaction as possible this weekend. | Decided to drive to Crater Lake. | With so little light pollution, I become very anxious. While Evan stared into the stars, I held my head in my hands. | | | | | | | | | | | | | | | | | | | | | | | | | | | | | | | | | | | | | | | | | | | | "You have to control yourself," Evan says, but I suspect that is not the problem. | Deep joy today, brought on by karaoke and the feeling of being loved widely. | Two snails on a swing set. | Puppet greets me at the door even in my most rotten moods. | Purchasing lightbulbs. | Cannot keep a single habit. | Said to Evan, "Monday shall not wake the mariner." He said, "Monody, Lu." And I stared at him confused. "The line is monody, Lu." | Dreamed last night of jewelry. | Would like to raise a child, would like to have already been raising a child. | Evan rinsed the wounds on my hand. | Nobody trusts me and I am despicable. | I breathe in to remember to breathe. | Doc asked today, "are you afraid of getting older?" and I said no, I have always longed for it. | Bought microwave. | Inside a peach, I found my mood. | In trouble at work. | I washed Puppet and cried. | I read all day. | | | | | | | | | | | | | | | | | | | | | | | | | | | | | | | | | | | | | | | | | | | | | | | | | | | | Bought new books and tried a different name for myself with the woman at the register. | | | Could stand to gain weight. | Realized I still have so many of those cheap face masks from the pharmacy. | Mark pulls a breath out of me. | | | | Am fighting less. Pulling myself back into patience. I think everyone is so sweet to me lately. | | | | | For Christmas, we are going to Evan's mother's home and I am painting her a picture of her lawn décor. | | Saw today a little girl pulling her friend's hair. | | | | Dreamed of high school in Fairfax, where everybody, even me, was a goat on wheels. | | | | | I told Evan I am terrified I will be this way forever. | | | I cooked tuna for the first time. | | | A younger cousin, who is very sick, is mailing me his collection of nickels. | | My neighbor practices the flute upstairs from noon to three, noon to three, noon to three. | | | | | | | I have no resolutions this year. I am walking in the park. "Look Lu," Evan points out, "hydrangeas."

DICTATION

QUIVERING DUVET PRESS, 2024

EDITORS' NOTE

The publication of *Dictation* in 2024 marks an obvious change in Montes-Torres's style, which carries through much of his late work. *Dictation* and *Hold Me to It* abandon the lyric short poem in favor of the long poem, embrace rigid and repetitive line forms, and mark a new pessimism in Montes-Torres's work. They are wordy, weighty, and often cynical books, but with a much more defined relation to the political than one finds in his early work.

Montes-Torres wrote *Dictation* sporadically over a period of five years, reaching 540 pages in its longest draft. Quivering Duvet Press, now famous for publishing Clarènce's *HOW DARE YOU* trilogy, but which was then a still-burgeoning independent press in Los Angeles, published *Dictation* at a still-intimidating 270 pages. At the time, Quivering Duvet was edited by Mia Axle, who met Montes-Torres at the library where he worked. Since *Dictation* is a rather unwieldy long poem in dozens of sections, we have decided to reproduce a short selection of its textures. The book was published in an edition of 300 and has never been reissued.

Few major events occur in Montes-Torres's life during the eleven years between *Sailing* and *Dictation*; instead, these years are marked by a slow but steady change in disposition. In 2015, Montes-Torres began to seek cognitive behavioral therapy to treat what he described to Bower as "thoughts scratching at the nape of my neck," which would occasionally shorten his temper and send him into outbursts. According to his journals from the period, he understood this as a worsening of depressive symptoms that he had faced since his late adolescence, though Bower considered his fits of anger to be a newer problem, believing that Montes-Torres's depression had improved in his middle age.

In his 20s, Montes-Torres was relatively private, did little to keep up with political events, and was often described as having his head in the clouds. He became more social during the most public era of his writing career, but was still considered by most a generally quiet, hermetic, and low-spirited man. However, after the failure of *Sailing* influenced him to take time away from public literary cultures, Montes-Torres gained an interest in following both current events and meteorology. From 2012-2026, Montes-Torres kept a blog where he forecast the weather and circuit court decisions of the following day. He would later share these predictions on his DODO stream, interspersing them with monologues from his favorite movies and reflections on his daily life. An obsession with water patterns *Dictation*, which Montes-Torres and Quivering Duvet edited and published in the context of the two great California fires of 2024. His blog extensively covered details of the fires, including predictions and potential preservation strategies for fire safety authorities. "Writing," he wrote in one blog, "is never made better by this, by devastation, by feeling that one is despicable, by this awfulness in the air. Regardless of what they tell you, art is never made better by all this."

FROM *DICTATION*

changing color of water
in response to the introduction
of chemicals
            an imprecise dictation
                        an icicle from the index finger
                        all the way to the brain

yellow color in water
in response to the introduction
of chemicals
            an imprecise dictation
                        an icicle from the index finger
                        all the way to the brain

increased levels of plastic in water
in response to the introduction
of plastic
            an imprecise dictation
                        an icicle from the index finger
                        all the way to the brain

decreased levels of fish in water
in response to the introduction
of chemicals
     an imprecise digitalization
         an icicle from the index finger
         that reaches towards but never reaches the brain

changing weight of water
in response to the introduction
of water
     an imprecise dictation
         an icicle from the water
         all the way to the brain

I saw salt in water
in response to the introduction
of salt in water
     an imprecise dictation
         an icicle from the index finger
         all the way to the brain

sound of water
call and response
with chemicals
      an imprecise dictation
            an icicle from the index finger
            all the way to the other index finger

changing color of water
in response to the introduction
of water into the city
      an imprecise dictation
            of what is hurting in the space
            between the finger and the brain

changing color of water
in response to the introduction
of water into the city
      dictation of the subway
            now covered
            in something like an icicle

the thought that water
will be akin to reading
or akin to chemicals
            an imprecise dictation
                        passing the index finger
                        over grass as it yellows

I watch a change of color
in response to the introduction
of chemicals
            dictation of the precipice
                        an icicle cutting the index finger
                        an icicle cutting the brain

changing span of water
in response to the introduction
of heat
            an imprecise dictation
                        no icicle
                        no brain

changing span of water
in response to the introduction
of heat
      the lie of dictation
            an icicle that takes the fault
            piercing the heel

decreased levels of oxygen in water
in response to the activity
of other animals
      an imprecise dictation
            the impatience between the hand
            that pulls the curtain and the curtain itself

decreased levels of plankton in water
in response to the introduction
of chemicals
      the eager disposition
            of the open mouth
            expecting plankton

boat along the water
where someone looks back
expectantly
    in response to
        chemicals, icicles, dictation
        "lost souls," salinization

changing color of water
as it rises
as it evaporates
    an imprecise dictation
        an icicle from the index finger
        all the way to brain

reflected in rising water
the gasp between clouds
an upside-down bird
    an imprecise dictation
        where an icicle
        is melted by days of rain

increasing levels of chemicals in water
the sound of a can
coming back to the shore
      an imprecise dictation
            an icicle from the index finger
            all the way to the brain

changing color of water
in response to the introduction
of chemicals
      an imprecise dictation
            an icicle from the index finger
            all the way to the brain

the sky over the canal
how I responded with anger
to what I saw floating in the water
      an imprecise dictation
            an icicle from the index finger
            all the way to the brain

I thought it was a mannequin

I thought it was a dog or something, a cat maybe

I thought it was a big bag

I thought it was some garbage

I thought it was driftwood

I thought it was a log burning

I thought it was a Halloween prank

I thought it was a tailor's dummy

I thought it was just someone passed out

I thought it was a joke

I thought it was debris

I thought it was a drunk person

I thought it was a dud

I thought it was a case with a handle on it

I thought it was an animal

I thought it was something you grabbed to get out of the water

I thought it was a big turtle on a log

I thought it was just the NyQuil

I thought it was all just part of the attraction

I thought it was a prop

I thought it was a doll

I thought it was a large rat

I thought it was a barrel

I thought I had seen him before

I thought it was a kid playing

I thought I was being tricked

I thought I was dreaming it

I thought it was a tree fallen over

I thought it was a stone

I thought it was impossible

I thought it was an alligator

I thought I was going to faint

I thought it was something else

I thought it was going to move eventually

I thought it was trash a neighbor threw in

I thought it must have been something plastic

I thought a fish had died or something

I thought it was someone swimming

I thought it was part of the scene

I thought it was a deer since it was by the road

I thought I was going to be sick

I thought it was just a puppet or something

I thought about my kids almost immediately

I thought it was maybe a sleeping bag

I thought it was teenagers messing around in the canal

it was like driving a long time

a cut on the left foot, just before the big toe

with a friend, maybe at night, and thinking together

a cut on the face, on the right cheek

in a form of quiet

a cut below the belly button

it was easier than I was told

a circular sore on the arm, maybe ringworm

and I quickly made myself scarce

a wide scrape above the right eye

imagined myself in a movie where I died

a deep gash in the left calf, which will require stitches

and came back again as steam, or as silicone

a beet-red rash going up the back to the nape of the neck

it was like driving a long time

a cut opening the right eye

I pictured my friend forgetting me

various scuff marks along both knees

I pictured a house floating on water

a deep, narrow wound on the left side reaching the diaphragm

I pictured rubbing alcohol poured into the canal

I cannot control
what I hear
or its relationship to
what you say

a bottle
buried in the sand
a receipt landed on
the pond
lily pads

I cannot separate
a siren from the pitches
it shifts between

hairspray picked up
by breeze, or a ziploc
bag cooked by the sun

your intentions are revealed
by the placement of your arms
I do everything but listen
I dream about the canal

snails on a swing set

If I put my hands in water

If I put my hands in water

If I put my hands in water

If I put my hands in water

If I put my hands in water

If I put my hands in water

If I put my hands in water

If I put my hands in water

If I put my hands in water

If I put my hands in water

If I put my hands in water

If I put my hands in water

If I put my hands in water

If I put your hands in tar

If I put your hands in tar

If I put your hands in tar

If I put your hands in tar

If I put your hands in tar

If I put your hands in tar

If I put your hands in tar

If I put your hands in tar

If I put your hands in tar

If I put your hands in tar

If I put your hands in tar

If I put your hands in tar

If I put your hands in tar

changing color of water
in response to the introduction
of chemicals
      an imprecise dictation
            unproven, obsessed with
            smoke over the city

changing weight of water
in response to the introduction
of weight
      an imprecise dictation
            unproven, obsessed with
            smoke over the city

churning between marble pillars
water responding
to its weight
      an imprecise dictation
            unproven, obsessed with
            smoke over the city

separation is impossible
in response to chemicals
to weight
       an imprecise dictation
              unproven, obsessed with
              smoke over the city

I see spots in my vision
lead and ice, tar and cream
awful weight
       an imprecise dictation
              unproven, obsessed with
              smoke over the city

something clear gaining color
in response to the introduction
of chemicals
       reddening
              unproven, obsessed with
              smoke over the city

HOLD ME TO IT

HALF-LIFE BOOKS, 2028

EDITORS' NOTE

While the couple's move to Philadelphia was occasioned by Evan Bower accepting a role in an artificial intelligence laboratory in Fishtown, Montes-Torres happily took the opportunity to leave his work at the library in Los Angeles. Though in his moments of fragility the predictability of his work had been comforting, in recent years that stability had corrupted into stagnation and frustration. For the first three years of their life in Philadelphia, Montes-Torres worked as a dog walker, notably for an exclusive breeder of golden retrievers, Laura Pinshickle Thompson, wife of the industrial developer Jensen Thompson.

Six months after moving to Philadelphia, motivated by the relative uneventfulness of the publication of *Dictation*, Montes-Torres began work on a new manuscript, which would become *Hold Me to It*. Continuing his interest in weather, Montes-Torres had become fascinated by the flooding and collapse of the New York City Subway system in early 2027, extensively documenting his thoughts on preventative measures for other cities on his blog. *Hold Me to It* is clearly influenced by this and other climate disasters of the 2020s in its fixation on the failures of infrastructure to cohere with the natural. Imagined as a kind of coda to the jeremiad that made up the previous book, *Hold Me to It* holds closely to themes of *Dictation*, and is again written in the form of the long poem. Less explicitly maximalist, however, the slim book only reaches sixty-five pages, published without front or back matter, excluding even a formal copyright page for its publisher, Half-Life Books.

The four editors of Half-Life Books began the press in 2026. They lived and worked together in Philadelphia in a polyamorous relationship consisting of ceramics professor Rebecca Reese, restauranteur Fratelli DiBruno, waste management activist Carmen Ina-Cabo, and human-interest journalist Joshua Leif, a friend to Montes-Torres from Leif's years in Los Angeles. Half-Life was dedicated to the publication of experimental poetic works and the mounting of catered art exhibitions in South Philadelphia. Leif solicited Montes-Torres for a manuscript in 2027 and Half-Life published *Hold Me to It* in March of 2028 in an edition of 300.

FROM *HOLD ME TO IT*

infrastructure has little capacity for promise making,

as we have all now learned,

though steadiness is its first and only appeal.

the idea is freckling on second consideration,

a bad reflection, as it always really was,

of the logical results of what we set out to do.

do not fantasize about atlantis, buried treasure,

when you were so baldly lied to

about what you could set your mind to

and disperse. a better version of a lily pad

is encoded in the current version of the lily pad.

return of the ice. fingers shaped into a gun.

the autumn of a philosopher, stuck.

be sure to watch the species in the other screen,

where colors are brighter and harder to track.

I go where I go. you rob me of my balance.

in a feature of august, the temptation is to fear

the heat that leads a melody, but in no way

is this behavior truly sane. you cannot sleep

with your head against a thesaurus when the promise

made was against variation in the name of something

dressed as innovation, which we now see as dishonest.

faulty patterning. in laying out where an object began

and another object ended, the promise reduced each

object to its lifespan. it circulated the bad news.

it said to be eager with your mind and its silhouette.

it saw pleasure as exhaustion's ricochet. it planted plants.

you hear that like I do, mosquitoes passing by your ear.

you hear that like I do, a third color

made in reference to two others,

set up just behind the stage.

everything about the golf course.

the end of all these minor acts within the diamond,

if that is how you would like to think of it,

but these are the returns.

the return to death, the conversation of all animals

in this new form of intimacy with our thoughts.

of course, water returns and reshelves.

I am handing out microscopic fires,

something you could silence

with the pinch of two fingers.

an island taken from its context,

skin peeled from a snake,

is a thin thing pulled apart by storms.

nothing could keep that word.

sun if it careens,

permit me to desire.

who is watching you as you run through the woods,

dirt scraping your thighs as they rush and sweat,

the taste of cocoa remaining just between your molars?

you invent a half-lion half-girl to rid you of this flu,

which is, in every case, a futile effort.

a dream from the head of st. eustace.

the promise absolved you of your genuine paranoia,

pretended that it was a system of roads.

you finally let the firefly out of your hand.

you watch as a friend makes a deep burn in his arm,

a promise that I still love you.

a world where the lily pad does not exist is programmed

into the current version of the lily pad.

there is so much discussion

around the behavior of the lie.

this time there is no thought of each other

or there is only thought of each other,

our holding here a honeybee as a forest burns

or the frightening moments when we think the same thing.

the promise is that all your senses are harvesters.

the milder anxieties will do you little good now

though they are unrelenting in their small constant need

as we are chest-deep in purchased horror.

I think singing to myself will guarantee me a next thought

though it barely does.

you speak

as if to fill this room with sound.

you barely fit into your clothes.

two mulch pieces rubbed together

will not start a fire.

a lithograph of a clover.

here and then I borrow your loneliness

as we watch the earth bite its lip and die.

this is what it can make of itself,

it bares its limit to you.

in sweetness pulled from a thorn,

the difference between belong and belong

in its least optimistic capacity.

every steady and silver handholding

an incomplete remark made on a bad bet.

except in loving you, I stupidly hope,

or except in taking a ruler to the ground.

when the stove is lit,

when I promise you anything,

hold me to it.

SOME SHIELDS

HALF-LIFE BOOKS, 2032

EDITORS' NOTE

On November 16th, 2029, Luis Montes-Torres stood in the middle of South and Broad St. in Philadelphia, linked at the waist to six golden retrievers, screaming insults and flicking bits of water ice at pedestrians and drivers alike. He was a one-man commotion, to be sure, but to the drivers he was a temporary nuisance and maybe even temporary entertainment. After an hour or so, three mounted police officers arrived on horses, spooking the six retrievers who set to running, dragging Montes-Torres across the asphalt and into the front end of an idling car. The irritated driver got out and fought with Montes-Torres while the police watched on, writing tickets. Montes-Torres was arrested but spent no time in jail; instead, he was hit with several fines and the loss of his dog walking job. The event, though its motivations were unclear, had clear consequences: it strained his finances, his relationship with Bower, and his relationship with himself.

His career now appeared to be—to him, at least—completely over, his previous two books but a sharp and final release of breath from a corpse. From late 2029 through most of 2030, he took a job at the Free Library of Philadelphia, nursed his wounds, and did not write a single poem. The pattern of aggression, anger, public fighting, and violent outbursts that had marked recent years became the central focus of his therapy and recovery.

"I am trying to do something, and I know I have to do it, not for Evan or for Puppet, but for me, since I have never found a reason in myself." This journal entry from November 2030 describes a turn from this recent nadir in Montes-Torres's health: the genesis of a meditation practice where he would go daily to the Wissahickon Valley Park, which had seen increased foot traffic after the closure of several state parks by the Pennsylvania Department of Conservation and Natural Resources in 2029. Unbothered by the plentiful hikers, Montes-Torres would stay there for several hours to sit and sing. "To clean my mind, to heal the Wissahickon," he writes, "the only thing that matters: to hear." At this point, with criticism of his work having all but disappeared, most of his early books now out of print, and scant book sales, Montes-Torres's attention had shifted away from his literary career. But his meditation represented a new way to access his writing and voice.

This practice was also a reaction, not to the condition of his career or mental health, but to the damage wrought by the flooding of Western Cuba, specifically in his birthplace of Pinar del Río. Montes-Torres closely followed news of the string of hurricanes in the Caribbean during early 2030, and the American immigration sanctions that followed. His journals make clear the connection between his meditation and these events, referring to his practice repeatedly as "private protest."

Though his meditation was not originally conceived in relation to his writing, in January of 2031, Montes-Torres began writing notes during his meditations towards a project that would become his last collection of poetry. *Some Shields* returns to the short poem as its organizing form, but foregoes the yearning of his early work. Half-Life press published *Some Shields* in 2032 with an introduction written by Joshua Leif. The introduction seems more an apologia for Montes-Torres as a somewhat frustrating and absent public figure than it seems a welcome to the new poems, perhaps in an effort to justify to readers his second publication with Half-Life. Initially published in an edition of 300, *Some Shields* received barely any critical attention, but was republished in 2046 to positive reviews by the Parisian press Mélasse Éditorial.

The Montes-Torres we get in *Some Shields* reminds us most of the Montes-Torres of *Hills and Towers*; he feels young, curious, quick. This doesn't feel like a last book, and it's likely Montes-Torres didn't plan for it to be. But even then, the speaker we get here is curiously reflective and wistful: on memories, on friends, on history, on the environment. Montes-Torres is actually out in the world here—a place he hasn't always been. Whether it sits well with him, whether he sits well with it—that is still somewhat unclear.

LUCKY COIN

reaching my hand across to dennis
I notice books he has been hiding from me
but cannot imagine giving up
a coca-cola on his dresser, a lucky coin
the way he speaks to me
when we are writing or when he asks
for advice on his lesson plans
it is the polar opposite of face blindness
when I have sweat coming down my ears
it is a sign I am getting better
at seeing my lion's image in a cloud
I depend very little on friendships but need them
nobody asks a whale the difference
between itself and the ice caps

A LETTER FROM SHARKEY TO AMES

these are the best fictional names
that I can convince myself are lovers

and if one writes to another
one might be forced to ask
how long it's been
since we've last seen each other
since the first pointed finger
knowing that my gum habit annoys you
all the weight we've lost or gained
this is the problem with letters
that I am so ferociously honest here
knowing I won't be in the room
when you read this and can
say the most divine things
about your patterns
the days we wasted
the thoughts I am still having
the sound you are making
I am weeping as I write this

and since I am in the business of making comparisons
I think that one's love for another
is like the egg in an egg cream
passed with obvious finesse
across the gingham table

A CASTLE, A SWORD, A KNIGHT

so far, I have lacked the confidence
to make any such claims on the importance
of fairy tales, though I know plenty of them
I pantomime the seven dwarves with my fingers
dancing them in the air
it's a question of proportions really
how I get to know you better
and the hawk we saw on the light pole
which reminded me to tell something
I cannot say I have had much exposure to
anything but the sound of the Wissahickon
and the endings of fairy tales
where sisters mutilate their toes
or a woman wakes up to a very pretty face

ON MOSS

these realizations I keep having
as I get older are becoming tiring
as they consistently remind me
of my poor shape
the subtle lilt in your speech
wood and felt slammed against timpani
in the park at night I whisper
an awful prophecy
I might die in the dark
I might feed a pigeon
regardless of who becomes
accustomed to this process
to these communications
and memorandums on fretting
I must preserve the mental image
of moss and the moss itself
the sound of water trickling past a stone
I am just so mad at you

THREE NOTES

what you hear now
the crackling of fire
keeps their engines running
sounds out prayers
to bad ideas

your knuckle scraped on the stone
has left an impression
or at least it has on me
since I realize now
I am thinking much clearer
at the sight of you bandaging
you've left quite the shock
in the hiking children too
who look as though
they've never seen blood
you set yourself up for failure
against a sky showing signs of rain

better answers come slower
between the first sound and the third
"utter devastation"
every moth here spreading a fine pink powder

ALLIANCE

it's in painting
that I solidify
my alliance
to research

the vibration
in my sternum
on singing a tritone
for salamanders

do any of you draw conclusions
when you walk on my hands
is it so easy to distinguish
between an hour and an idea
are all my thoughts repulsive

I find in trust a magnet
to draw all the awe in
look fast to my left
at a crying blond
maybe for joy

the belly is a shrine

become the sail or its wind

IN MY BEST ATTIRE

a white truck turned over on a highway
a brilliant black stain
regardless I put no value in this
this picaresque put on by pests
plastic and metal the bird's first death
in my best attire I seem exactly like
a swamp to which one sends tawdry letters
a place for forgetting and remembering
you draw an eye over my eye
you pull a coin from behind my ear
one must forgive their father
this lesson I learned hanging by the foot
blood rushing to my head
one must dress better
as one is being pushed into a crowd
of loved ones all the time
the image of yesterday
is an impression in the face
from sleeping too long on your hand
everyone is still alive
everyone would like to be a tuxedo

FLOOD MAP, PINEWOOD

a tobacco plant submerged
its flowers cut and released
into burning water
it begins the question of prehistory
I think I know you from somewhere
I think I should at least
all this replacement
you push my glasses up
along the bridge of my nose
ask where we "seem"
I know a better way
a system of caves
tricked into believing
that there is a human face
in these dolomite hills

ENDEAVORS

I get a dreadful worry
about blue lights, money, the mail
and this feeling sits in me a long time
like pear slices in their juice
as my friend tells me a story
of all his recent endeavors
which somehow gets to rumors of the wendigo
but it doesn't get worse
in fact I get to picturing
time spent with my friend
picturing the time we're spending now
and I tell him
to start the story over
because I wasn't really listening

METHOD OF LOCI

how do I remember your name
when the noise of the land
is a scrambled half-prayer
sounding loud and high
I put it in a house in my mind
though palpating the air in the dark
for a sign some noise a ligature
everything is clear
every year is drawn together
like the bends in a paper fan
I touch my pinky to the soil
I almost think to sleep
a child is wishing on a pond
for a girl's attention
there is no reason to take notes
no one has ever lied
an oil painting of a field
with a detail of me
forgetting all my life

LAST POEMS

EDITORS' NOTE

Luis Montes-Torres died in his sleep on April 11th, 2035, from complications related to brain cancer. He lived with the illness for eleven months.

After the publication of *Some Shields*, he wrote only three poems, none of which saw publication. They are printed here in their entirety for the first time.

TODAY

tomorrow's fog is perpendicular to my idea of ordered surprise
it's everything we've refused to say out loud

today, I said grace over my meal
wondering about the cold front coming in

if I'm being honest, this entire conversation
brings up my most belabored memories

> missing the point
> joking that I celebrate certainty
> wanting more
> kissing you on the forehead
> worrying about the dog

a diorama of our home answers the easiest questions
and I put little faith in this poem's ability to solve the others

I see you are counting in your head
it's a drip of oil
it's what I already know

ATTACHMENT AND AMBIVALENCE

Wander with me, between water and water,
as a program we use to gently suggest a set
of ramifications, two isolated owls, for the actions
that led to this, to you sitting beside me,
and you will cease to wince at every mention of the name.

The leaf, cutting the sky from the sky, at least for a moment,
implies ambivalence drowned in light. A particle
of an unknown element, which travels a breath between us,
and strikes fear into a mother's heart; it is not just
some fairy dust, not just the silent operations of aliens.

I never made light of difference, I reduced it to lawns
moving slowly, the syrup the animals wade through,
the dialogue of two agents in disagreement. Forecasting
by waving my wand over a pile of my bones, I say a picture
is like a portrait, and that in some way I will get my mulligan.

As a little courtesy, don't say you need me, pare the rind
off of that starfruit, find an upside in calculus. Get cold
in the space between your freckles; look out the window.
If I am right to guess, you already know what I am going to say next,
and you know it is the perfect compliment.

TROPICAL NEGATIVE

keep your eye trained
to the matador
in this subplot.
in my talkative history
how much has crumbled?
what can next burn in some
one else's life, thousands of years
down the line, when threats
resurface as dreams?
the diameter of what I have done.
I am watching you
set a match to my home.
I move every
body in this tradition.
absorbing the elegant
foreigner in a wisecrack
against the world, you
treat me as your ghostwriter.
I click my heels
against a hemisphere.
I am ignorant in my best dreams.
tropical negative,
recorded as an injection of comedy.
do not tell your
analyst, but I was
born for this.
the sun's advantage.
my only preference.
at a time like this,
what to say? what to say?
gamma ray! gamma ray!

Everything past this page can be assumed to be true.

ACKNOWLEDGEMENTS

Madness was born out of the immense pain, loss, change, and joy shared during the last years of the 2010s with my husband Jibreel Powell, for whom I am profoundly grateful. It is also born out of the cultural context my family and I inhabit. I am ever grateful for our story. I am specifically grateful here for the stories of my father and uncle, Francisco and Gustavo Ojeda, brothers now passed on.

Madness is in no way an autobiography, but it is in many ways a simulation of my own struggles with my mental health. During several mental crises I faced during the last years of the 2010s, I absorbed art and aesthetics with an insatiable hunger and with steady optimism. There is some art that I interacted with heavily during the writing of this book that must be mentioned in acknowledgement: the music and writing of Sebastian Castillo (from whom the image of the icicle and brain comes), the music of Arthur Russell, the poetry of Roberto Harrison, the poetry of Reinaldo Arenas, the poetry of Raquel Salas Rivera, the poetry of John Ashbery, the writing and teaching of Lauren Berlant, Roland Barthes's *A Lover's Discourse*, the journals of Lou Sullivan, the writing and teaching of C. Riley Snorton, the fiction of Manuel Puig, the poetry of James Schuyler, and the poetry of Alfred Starr Hamilton. These people and many more taught me about love and about madness.

I am thankful for my friends and family who have listened to me think this book out loud, and perhaps even encouraged its writing, especially Nash Jenkins, who (after Jibreel) probably tolerated the most unsolicited updates on this book's progress and trip-ups. I am also thankful to the intellectual community at the University of Chicago who, often unknowingly, have sharpened this book's thought, especially Adam Fales who was the first colleague of mine to hear its "plot" (relayed over lemony cocktails).

The death of Kevin Killian caused a turn in this book's writing. To his friendship and writing I am greatly indebted. During the editing stage of this book, another great teacher of mine, Lauren Berlant, also passed away. Though I never spoke of *Madness* to either Kevin or Lauren, both of their thinking is deeply embedded in its pages.

Poems from this book were published by the following journals or series: *Elderly*, Alina Pleskova's Sitting Room Series, *the tiny*, *PoetryNow*, *Spoon River Poetry Review*, *Texas Review*, *Aurochs*, *JuxtaProse*, *EOAGH*, *Tripwire*, and *bedfellows' Little Black Book of Bedfellows*. Six poems from the "Hills and Towers" section were published as a chapbook by TENDE/RLOIN on the occasion of AWP 2019. This chapbook was titled *A Change in Me*. My sincere appreciation goes to these publishing bodies for giving *Madness* its first version of life in the world.

Thanks to the Nightboat Books team in total, and especially Lindsey Boldt, Stephen Motika, Caelan Nardone, Andrea Abi-Karam, Tal Milovina, and Gia Gonzales for all their conversations and support of this book. Lindsey's editing has been integral towards making this book what it is today. Thanks also to Joel Gregory for their design work; if you are a publisher and you don't hire Joel, you are a fool!

I hold the poetry communities of Philadelphia, Chicago, and Miami in my heart.

This book is of immigrants and their children.

Gabriel Ojeda-Sagué is a poet and writer living in Chicago. He is the author of three other books of poetry, most recently including *Losing Miami* (2019), which was nominated for the 2020 Lambda Literary Award in Gay Poetry. He is also the co-editor of a book of selected sketches by the artist Gustavo Ojeda and the author of chapbooks on Cher, The Legend of Zelda, and anxious bilingualism. He is currently a PhD candidate in English at the University of Chicago where he works in the study of sexuality.

NIGHTBOAT BOOKS

Nightboat Books, a nonprofit organization, seeks to develop audiences for writers whose work resists convention and transcends boundaries. We publish books rich with poignancy, intelligence, and risk. Please visit nightboat.org to learn about our titles and how you can support our future publications.

The following individuals have supported the publication of this book. We thank them for their generosity and commitment to the mission of Nightboat Books:

Kazim Ali
Anonymous (4)
Abraham Avnisan
Jean C. Ballantyne
The Robert C. Brooks
   Revocable Trust
Amanda Greenberger
Rachel Lithgow

Anne Marie Macari
Elizabeth Madans
Elizabeth Motika
Thomas Shardlow
Benjamin Taylor
Jerrie Whitfield &
   Richard Motika

This book is made possible, in part, by grants from the New York City Department of Cultural Affairs in partnership with the City Council and the New York State Council on the Arts Literature Program.